Spike Likes Ham

by Alaina Kim
illustrated by Hannah Graff

Practice Decodable 23

Mc Graw Hill Education

Bothell, WA • Chicago, IL • Columbus, OH • New York, NY

MHEonline.com

Send all inquiries to:
McGraw-Hill Education
8787 Orion Place
Columbus, OH 43240

ISBN: 978-0-02-144763-3
MHID: 0-02-144763-2

Printed in the United States of America.

7 8 9 CTM 23

We Had Ham

Dad gave ham to Spike.
Spike ate it.

Spike stared at Mom.
Mom gave him ham.

Liz and Dave did the same.

All the kids did.

Spike sat and ate.

Spike Had Ham

"Do we have ham left?" said Dad.

"We do not," said Mom.

Spike ate it all!

Spike likes to have ham.
Spike likes ham a lot.